AF472036

Beats Below the Rust Belt

Collected Freeform Verse

By: C.R. Asher

Printed in the USA.

ISBN 978-1-329-39738-5

Dedicated to The Free, Fallen, Heartsick, Homeless, Hurting, Dreamers, Dispossesed, Distraught, and Downtrodden, Lovers, and most importantly - You, The reader.

"My belt holds my pants up, but the belt loops hold my belt up. I don't really know what's happening down there. Who is the real hero?" - Mitch Hedberg

Credits:

Art:	*C.R. Asher*
Editing:	*C.R. Asher*
Layout:	*C.R. Asher*
Cover:	*C.R. Asher*

To all my readers, Old and new; Thanks for your support.

Regards,

C.R. Asher

Contents

Advice

Give me knowledge.

Tell me things.

Let me understand.

I seek your approval.

Learning dysfunctions.

Rational disabilities.

Keep me from advancing.

But damned if I don't try.

Improvement is the goal.

Repetition the key.

Good is well enough.

But I'd rather be better.

Audial

Sometimes I hear things.
Voices that make no sense.
Saying random snippets.
Nothing comes in clear.
But I still sadly hear.
All that they gotta say.
Much to my sweet dismay.
I wonder how much of it's me.
From which they are speaking.
Or is the convo about me?
If so they should speak up.
Otherwise they are being rude.
Or is it just me?

Conjure

I conjecture.

Irrelevant.

Gallavant.

Here and there.

To and fro.

Like the wind.

Always go.

Passover me.

Stricken down.

Unwashed clown.

In the moment.

Head of coven.

First to come.

Last to see.

Love and leave.

Heart on sleeve.

Pants unleashed.

Until deceased.

Disregard

Start the day with a good outlook.

Make a conscious decision to do something.

Set on organizing things around the house.

Spend the day indoors clearing out closets.

Build some more walls for my unecessary things.

Trade in the cleaning supplies for some yard tools.

A day spent in the garden improves the environment.

Getting your hands in the dirt is a grounding experience.

Do something functional to keep the blood flowing.

The freedom of not giving a shit is liberating.

So everyone should just try it sometime.

Subject yourself to catharsis.

Or do something.

Embers

I've got a book of matches.

Kept it since I was a child.

Laying on a table at a restaurant.

That my parents took me to one time.

Bright, and new when I first took it.

A folded sleeve of infinite possibilities.

But only I knew it's true secret.

To be lit when the world went dark.

I lit one when I got real sick.

I lit another when my parents split.

And another when the last one abandoned me.

Whenever everything felt like the end.

I struck one of my magic matches.

I was reminded that there is always hope.

Then I met you, and they grew obsolete.

Until you left with no explanation.

I pulled the pack out of my cache.

Next to the letters and notes you wrote.

I freed a match, the final one, and struck.

Now it is almost done, and I concluded -

Sometimes old flames just need to go out.

Gone

I woke up.

You were gone.

I just closed my eyes.

Only for a moment.

Opened them in disbelief.

Choked on my grief.

You were gone.

I felt gravity.

Then I felt misery.

Turned my guts inside out.

Drained the last bit dry.

Now I can't feel much at all.

You were gone.

Not even a single tear.

A halfhearted goodbye.

Said some things.

I can't take back.

Needed your love.

But I'm not the one.

Your heart chose.

I looked so hard.

Prayed for an eternity.

For such a long time.

Forgive me I'm not me.

Without you, you see?

As your memory fades.

I go along with it.

I've become alone.

I woke up.

You were gone.

Means

Sometime I think too much.

Read all the wrong things.

I'm into some bad concepts.

Furthering terrible notions.

Bordering the inappropriate.

The problem with that is means.

But I'm always willing to change.

Though I'm not very proud of it.

Honestly why do I do anything?

I'm very keen on uncommon sense.

I thrive well enough on medocrity.

Striving in the midwest wasteland.

Sometimes freedoms are limited.

No past in the christmas present.

The birth daze is never trivial.

You better get it when you can.

Neptune

The water looks cold.

But I'll dive right in.

I expect to drown.

Even though I can float.

What lies in store for me.

Under the deep blue sea.

Davey Jones locker?

The rest of the Monkee's?

Sailing in uncharted waters.

A son of unknown fathers.

The pirates life for me.

I'll take it if it's free.

That's who I aim to be.

No idea, I.D., just belief.

Triton's graces in relief.

No Offense

The lies you told.

I chose to believe.

Complete trickery.

In spite of my heart.

Telling me otherwise.

I risked a total mutiny.

Of thought, and reason.

A miniature self treason.

To let you affect me.

Shortly, then reject me.

I should have listened.

When my guts insisted.

But I was too busy,

Being sappily in love.

Or so I had thought.

You tore out my heart.

So to make some amends.

Offer no more offense.

I've given up listening.

To the sounds left within.

Gone deaf to my chagrin.

Silence echoes in the haze.

Where my heart used to stay.

Beating with dual regularity.

Now lost in a solemn singularity.

On the Beach

The air was cool, but tolerable on the beach.

Looking out into a shifting slate grey sky,

I was lost in the moment.

Still am.

But I knew somewhere out there a storm was

brewing. I knew it because the same thing

was happening inside me.

Like knows like.

I have always been one to be easily pleased
with the simple things. But at some point
I grew dissatisfied with everything.

But not there.

I watched the waves come in, and go out.
My heart calmed. I laid there next to you
hoping to just stay there forever.

I could breathe.

Almost everything about you gave me peace.
But I felt your departure since your arrival.
As I still do.

And will for the unseen future.

I can picture the people passing by. I can smell the salty air. I can see the myriad colors in the setting sun that was in the sky.

I could even picture you happy too.

I can count every shell. I can feel every grain of sand. I can see every inch of you. But I can't feel you anymore.

And it's like losing a limb.

I gave all I had. I did it, and would again. But I have nothing left. And someone else has you.

I've never been good at letting go.

In my mind I never left that beach. But I keep that part locked in the back of my head.

I keep you there too.

So I can't go there, unless I am willing to stay. Like in a final destination type of thing.

I am not afraid.

And by that I mean leave what's left of me behind, forever. I have things to do so I can't yet, but soon.

I hope so.

One day I will return. I'll be able to stay.

Then maybe I'll be pleased easily again.

Paces

Every day is ritual.

I wake up.

Stretch.

Meditate.

Drink soda.

Deficate.

Urinate.

Work.

Work.

Work some more.

Think about yesterday.

Have little wars in my head.

Work.

Work.

Work some more.

Eat.

Drink.

Consume media.

Work some more.

Medicate.

Lay down.

Speak to ghosts.

Work.

Work.

Work some more.

Sleep if lucky.

I'm not good at sustaining things.

I really need a vacation.

Safe And Warm

I'm looking for a room.

Want to lay my troubles down.

Relax and let the world melt.

All my work is near done.

It has stopped being fun.

I just want to call it a day.

This is not alot to ask for.

A spot to rest my old bones.

Some place to call my own.

Release me from the grief.

Just let me go to sleep.

Lay my head down, not to roam.

Ground I can call my home.

Steps

I'm sick of this broken step,

It serves no purpose, but to injure.

It once worked so very well,

Or at least I'd like to figure.

Can it be mended, or repaired?

Corrected of its errors?

Given a new and focused life?

Instead of being a source of strife?

Is it too much for me to ask?

Too complex of a task?

Or a metaphor for my pain?

A revelation all too plain?

Someone please tell me?

From this step will I be free?

Or is the job just up to me?

Strain

Hard to remember.

Tough to forget.

Issues with vices.

Living in regret.

Look to the future.

Live in the past.

Ready to gamble.

The dice have been cast.

I don't have much.

But I do got alot.

It's all that I have.

Until it just rots.

Tough to remember.

Hard to forget.

Living with vices.

Issues in regret.

The Extent

Don't sleep much.

Eat only when I have to.

Take aspirin to thin my blood.

Pop painkillers to dull the pain.

Swallow whiskey to kill the memories.

So what can I do for the anger?

Just pray that it doesn't get free?

Innately hostile by my virtue.

Arising whenever innapropriate.

I never feel that signifigant.

Always representing the other.

You start the journey one way.

Sometimes ending it in another.

So piss or get off the pot.

The best me that I can be.

To the extent of my ability.

About the Author:

A veteran, and connoisseur of long nights, rough days, warm taverns, and cold beds - C.R. Asher is a man of many skills, and few talents. Born in a small town in the Midwest, He has traveled a lot of the eastern U.S., and someday hopes to continue on westward like the pioneers of old.

A gentleman of renaissance, his interests include writing, sketching, and playing music on his beat up accoustic. Wherever cold beer is served, karaoke booms, or the jukebox plays steadily in the backdrop you are likely to find him, at least in spirit.